# Body Talk

# Control Freak

## HORMONES, THE BRAIN AND THE NERVOUS SYSTEM

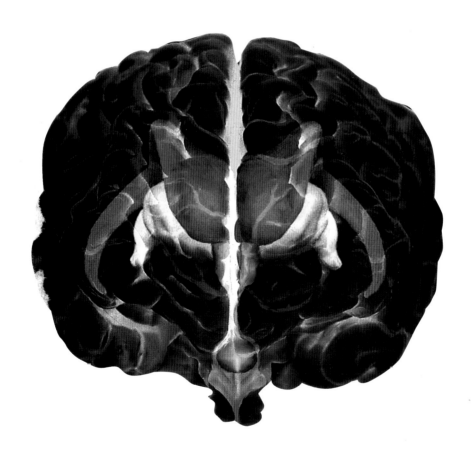

Steve Parker

# www.raintreepublishers.co.uk

Visit our website to find out more information about **Raintree** books.

To order:
☎ Phone 44 (0) 1865 888113
🖹 Send a fax to 44 (0) 1865 314091
💻 Visit the Raintree bookshop at **www.raintreepublishers.co.uk**
to browse our catalogue and order online.

First published in Great Britain by Raintree,
Halley Court, Jordan Hill, Oxford, OX2 8EJ, part
of Harcourt Education.
Raintree is a registered trademark of Harcourt
Education Ltd.

© Harcourt Education Ltd 2006
First published in paperback in 2007
The moral right of the proprietor has been
asserted.

Editorial: Melanie Waldron, Rosie Gordon,
and Megan Cotugno
Design: Philippa Jenkins, Lucy Owen,
and John Walker
Illustrations: Darren Linguard and Jeff Edwards
Picture Research: Mica Brancic and
Ginny Stroud-Lewis
Production: Chloe Bloom
Originated by Dot Gradations Ltd, UK
Printed and bound in China by South China
Printing Company

10-digit ISBN: 1 406 20062 X (hardback)
13-digit ISBN 978 1 4062 0062 1
10 09 08 07 06
10 9 8 7 6 5 4 3 2 1

10 digit ISBN 1 406 20068 9 (paperback)
13 digit ISBN 978 1 4062 0068 3
11 10 09 08 07
10 9 8 7 6 5 4 3 2 1

**British Library Cataloguing in
Publication Data**
Parker, Steve
Control freak! : hormones, the nervous system
and the brain. - (Body talk)
1.Nervous system - Juvenile literature
2.Hormones -
Juvenile literature
I.Title
612.8
A full catalogue record for this book is available
from the British Library.

**Acknowledgements**
The publishers would like to thank the following
for permission to reproduce photographs:
Action Plus **p. 40** (Glyn Kirk), **p. 6** (Mike Hewitt),
**p. 8** (Neil Tingle); Alamy **pp. 36-37, 21**
(Kolvenbach), **p. 19** (Profimedia. CZ s.r.o.);
Corbis **pp. 6-7, 18-19, 34-35; 20** (Bob Gelberge),
**pp. 4-5** (George Hall), **pp. 16-17** (Lawrence
Manning), **p. 29** (Michael Kevin Daly), **p. 22**
(Rolf Bruderer), **p. 27** (Varie/Alt), **p. 35** (Creatas);
Getty Images **pp. 20-21; 10** (Joe McNally), **pp.
28-29** (Image Bank), **pp. 12, 37** PhotoDisc), **pp.
5, 5, 24-25, 33, 40-41** (Stone),**p. 43** (Taxi);
Harcourt Education/Tudor Photography **pp. 15,
30-31**; Science Photo Library **pp. 42; 10-11, 22-
23** (AJ Photo), **p. 14** (CNRI), **pp. 26-27** (Dr M.A.
Ansary), **pp. 23, 39** (James Holmes), **p. 39**
(Michael Donne),**p. 9** (Pasieka), **pp. 32-33** (TEK
Image), **p. 38** (Zephyr), **pp. 12-13** (Superstock).

Cover photograph of head with wires
reproduced with permission of Tips.

The author and publisher would like to thank
Ann Fullick for her assistance in the preparation
of this book.

The paper used to print this book comes from
sustainable resources.

Disclaimer
All the Internet addresses (URLs) given in this
book were valid at the time of going to press.
However, due to the dynamic nature of the
Internet, some addresses may have changed, or
sites may have ceased to exist since publication.
While the author and publishers regret any
inconvenience this may cause readers, no
responsibility for an such changes can be
accepted by either the author or the publishers.

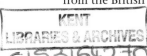
612.8

Dedicated to the memory of Lucy Owen

# Contents

Any words appearing in the text in bold, **like this**, are explained in the glossary. You can also look out for them in 'Body language' at the bottom of each page.

# Total control

You are blasting through the sky in a supersonic jet plane, travelling at incredible speed – the length of three soccer pitches every second!

You need total concentration and razor-sharp **senses**. Your eyes dart about the dials and controls, checking engine power and fuel levels. Your hands feel the control stick and your body detects the plane's every twist and turn.

Through the headset, your ears monitor messages from your commander back at base. Your mouth is dry and you feel the "buzz" of **adrenaline** as your heart thumps and your muscles tense.

## Body machine checklist

✔ **Sensors** – eyes, ears, nose, tongue, skin

✔ Hard drive and central processer – brain

✔ Download – **nerves** carry signals from sensors to brain

✔ Upload – nerves take signals from brain to muscles

✔ Life long guarantee – substances called **hormones** control growth and inner body processes

With the roar of the ➤ jets, the pilot's senses are extra-alert and his brain is in complete command.

**adrenaline**   a hormone that gets the body ready for action

## The brain in the plane

All this information from your senses feeds into the main control centre for the plane – your brain. Every second, you decide about your speed, height, and direction. You are so highly trained that you hardly have to think about some of this. Your brain seems to have its own "automatic pilot". In fact, your brain has to control one amazing and complex machine – your body – so that your body can control another incredible and complicated machine – the plane.

As you fly such a fast, powerful and dangerous jet with supreme skill, you really need to be ... a control freak!

**Find out later ...**

*What is your brain doing while you are asleep?*

*Why do children and adults like different flavours?*

*What happens when you are scared?*

**hormone**   substances made by hormonal or endocrine glands, which spread around the body in the blood, and affect or control body parts

# Control centre

## Use it, don't lose it

The soft, delicate brain is well shielded by the hard **skull** bone around it. But sometimes the brain needs extra protection, like a helmet or hard-hat. It is important to wear good protection whenever you take part in activities like climbing a rock face or cycling. In extreme sports such as tobogganing (right), a helmet is essential!

If you could see your brain, you might not be impressed. It is a dome-shaped lump that looks like pinky-grey jelly, and weighs about one and a half kilograms. It has deep grooves and wrinkles over its surface, and a stalk at the base.

But your brain is the most exciting place you can imagine. It is where you think, have ideas, store memories, decide to take actions, control movements, work out problems, daydream, worry, and have feelings like sadness, excitement, and joy. It is the place where your personality comes alive. In many ways, your brain is YOU.

Medical scanner machines ➤ show a living, working brain. Around it are thin cushion-like layers called **meninges**, which help to protect it.

**blood glucose** sugar obtained from the breakdown of sugars and other carbohydates in food - the body's main source of energy

## Big or small?

Have you got a big head? Like other body parts, brains vary in size and shape from person to person. But there is no link between brain size and cleverness or intelligence. Otherwise some creatures would be much smarter than us. The sperm whale has the world's biggest brain – the size of a suitcase. But as far as we know, it is not a genius! It is what you do with your brain, rather than its size, that is important.

The more you use your brain by thinking and remembering, the faster and more accurate you will become at these processes. Just as physical exercise can increase your muscle power, mental exercise like learning and solving problems can increase your brain power.

brain          meninges

### DID YOU KNOW?
Overall, the body is about 65 per cent water. But the brain is even more watery; about 75 per cent. If you could squash a brain like a sponge, you would squeeze out enough water to fill a one-litre juice carton.

**meninges**   three thin layers around the brain and spinal cord, which protect and nourish them. They are called the dura mater, arachnoid, and pia mater

## Where did you get that idea?

Your brain has several main parts, each doing different jobs, but all joined so they work together. The biggest part is the large wrinkled dome on top, the **cerebrum**. It makes up more than three-quarters of the whole brain. This is where you have most of your thoughts and ideas, and where you understand information from your eyes, ears and other **senses**.

## Super skills

When you learn skilful movements, you are using your **cerebellum**. This is the rounded, wrinkled part at the brain's lower rear. It makes your muscles move with split second control.

▼ The brain is very complicated, with many parts doing different jobs – but they all work together brilliantly.

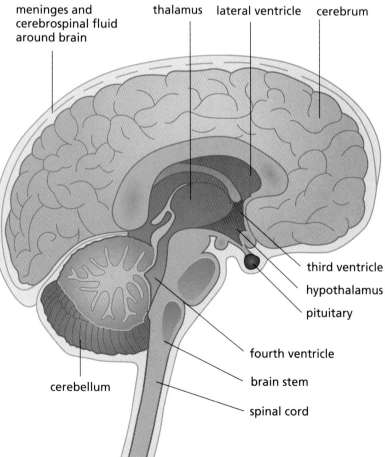

meninges and cerebrospinal fluid around brain

thalamus    lateral ventricle    cerebrum

third ventricle

hypothalamus

pituitary

fourth ventricle

brain stem

spinal cord

cerebellum

**cerebellum**   part at the rear of the brain, which controls muscle actions
**cerebrum**   large upper portion of the brain with "white matter" inside and a surface layer of "grey matter"

## Inner parts

Are you feeling wide-awake, or tired and sleepy? In the middle of the brain is a part shaped like two eggs, the **thalamus**. This helps to control your awareness, from fully alert to daydreaming, feeling tired or fast asleep. It also helps to pass information coming in from the senses to the huge cerebrum above.

## Small but important

When did you last feel really hungry, very thirsty, or have strong emotions like anger or great joy? All these feelings are based in a part just below the thalamus, called the **hypothalamus**. It is only as big as a grape, but it has huge effects on the way you behave.

## Hollow heads

Did you know that your brain is hollow? Inside it are four small chambers, called **ventricles**, filled with a pale yellow liquid – **CSF,** or **cerebrospinal fluid.** CSF covers the outside of the brain too. As it slowly flows, it brings nourishment to the brain, and takes away waste. Of course, like other body parts, the brain has a blood supply, to bring nourishment and remove wastes.

## Brain bricks

All body parts are made of microscopic "building blocks" called **cells**. The brain's cells are called **nerve cells**. Each has long "arms" that almost touch those of other nerve cells (below). They pass on tiny electrical signals called nerve messages.

### TOO MANY TO IMAGINE

- There are more than 100,000,000,000 microscopic nerve cells in the brain. That's 100 billion.

- Each is linked to thousands of others, so the connections between all the nerve cells number trillions of trillions.

- Every day up to 10,000 brain cells die. But that's normal. There are so many cells left, it hardly matters.

## No-pain brain!

The brain has no touch or pain **sensors**, so it can't feel anything – even the knife of a brain surgeon. Amazingly people can be wide-awake during a brain operation (below). However parts around the brain do have pain sensors, so an injection is given to numb the area.

## Think!

Every time you look, listen, feel, read, write, and move – you use your **cerebral cortex**. This is the name for the thin covering of the brain's main part, the **cerebrum**. Spread out, the cortex would be about as large as a pillowcase – and almost as thin. But it has lots of deep folds and wrinkles so it fits inside your **skull**. Each area of the cortex has a special task, as you'll see later.

Nerve messages pass around the brain ▼ as tiny electrical signals. Sensor pads on the skin detect these faint signals, and show them as wavy or spiky lines called an **EEG (electro-encephalogram)** – real "brain waves"!

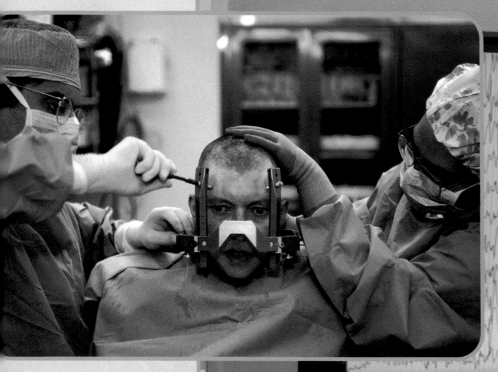

**axon**    part of a nerve cell (neuron) that takes messages from the main nerve cell body to other nerve cells or muscles or glands
**dendrites**    parts that take messages from nerve cells to the main cell body

## Grey and white

The cortex is the main place for our thoughts, decisions and awareness – what we call our "mind".

The cortex is made of billions of **nerve cells** linked together by their spider-like "arms", or **dendrites**. Every second these carry millions of messages. The cortex is coloured grey and is sometimes called "grey matter".

Underneath the cortex is "white matter", which makes up most of the inside of the cerebrum. This contains long wire-like parts from nerve cells, known as nerve fibres or **axons**. The fibres link the nerve cells of the cortex to other parts of your brain.

### Left or right?

The main brain has two halves, called **cerebral hemispheres**. These look similar but work differently. The left side deals with words, numbers, scientific skills and working through problems. The right side deals with shapes, colours, sounds, music, imagination and ideas. Which one do you use most?

"It was the darkest, blackest night I could remember. Far away, an owl hooted. A car roared past, and I smelled its exhaust fumes. Suddenly, a huge flash of lightning lit up the street, and a giant clap of thunder shook the earth ..."

**Can you see, hear, smell and feel this story? You only need the words. Then your mind, imagination and memory take over.**

**sensor** part which detects something, like light, sound, or the level of a certain substance inside itself, and sends messages to the brain

## Brain drain

The brain keeps short-term memories for just a few minutes or hours. These are usually less important, like texting a quick message or what we ate for lunch. Soon we forget them. Otherwise the brain would be full of unimportant information.

## Memories are made of ... what?

Can you remember a recent happy time like your birthday, a holiday or a fun day out? Take a short time to bring back those memories. Are they just sights or scenes? Or can you also remember sounds, smells, and perhaps your feelings too?

The more you think back, the more you can remember. This shows memories are more complicated than they seem.

## The nerve message pathways

But what are memories? Your brain has billions of microscopic **nerve cells** linked together in trillions of ways, to carry nerve messages. A memory is probably a set of links that carry a nerve message along a certain path.

Our strongest memories are ➤ usually exciting or strange events – times that have seemed very good, very bad, or very scary!

hippocampus   part inside the brain that is important for memory

Each time you recall the memory, the nerve message goes along its path from one nerve cell to the next, and the links stay fresh.

So using a memory often, by thinking about an event, keeps the paths open and the links strong. Memories that aren't used much fade away, the links are lost – and you forget.

## Memory centres

Memories are stored in several parts of the brain. These include the main **cortex** over the top, and also parts inside like the **hippocampus**. How would you remember a word like hippocampus? Would there be strange pictures on this memory's pathway – like a hippo in a tent?

**QUIZ**

Look at these pictures for 20 seconds. Then close the book and try to draw them. Which is easiest to copy? Probably the right-hand one.

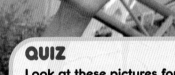

Both pictures have the same parts. But the right one has a familiar pattern that means something, making it easier to remember.

# The body's intranet

## What a nerve!

Your main nerve is the **spinal cord**, carrying information between your brain and your body. It runs from the base of your brain, down inside the bones of your neck and back. All the way down it, 31 pairs of nerves branch off to your various body parts.

The internet is made up of the links between millions of computers all around the world. Countless messages pass around this network every second. The body has lots of information passing around inside it too.

The brain receives and sends out messages all the time, to control body parts and make sure they work together. This information is in the form of tiny electrical signals called nerve messages. They pass along wire-like parts called **nerves**, which link the brain to all body parts. This system of nerves is like the body's own inner network or "intranet".

base of brain

skin on back of neck

- brain
- spinal cord
- radial nerve
- sciatic nerve
- tibial nerve

The body's nerves go from the ▲ brain and its main nerve, the spinal cord, to every part. The nerves branch smaller and smaller, right into the fingertips and ends of the toes.

windpipe   back bones   spinal cord

**nerve**   string-like part that carries messages around the body as tiny pulses of electricity

## Comings and goings

Nerves look like pieces of shiny, bendy, grey string. Inside each nerve is a bundle of **nerve fibres**, much thinner than hairs. These are the long, wire-like parts of **nerve cells** that carry nerve messages.

Your brain knows what the messages mean, because of where they come from. For example, messages from tiny touch **sensors** in your hand tell you that you are holding this book.

### GET ON YOUR NERVES

- If all the nerves in your body could be joined end to end, they'd stretch around the world twice.
- Your thickest nerve is your **sciatic nerve**, in your upper leg, which is about as wide as your thumb.
- Your spinal cord is about as thick as your little finger.
- One of the shortest main nerves, only the length of your thumb, is from your eye to your brain.

### Pins and needles

If you sit or lie awkwardly for a while, you may feel a horrible tingling or buzzing, known as "pins and needles". This may happen because a nerve is squashed. As soon as you rub and stretch, the nerve gets back to normal and the feeling goes away.

## Info in and out

Every second, your brain receives and sends millions of messages along the nerve pathways. Some of your nerves, like the one from each eye, only carry messages one way, into the brain. They are **sensory nerves**.

Other nerves only carry messages from your brain to your muscles. The nerve to the voicebox in your neck does this, so that you can speak. These are called **motor** nerves.

Some nerves carry messages both ways, like the nerve to your tongue, so your brain can recognise the tastes there and also tell your tongue to move. These are known as mixed nerves.

### What happens where?

The brain's outer layer or cortex looks the same all over. But different areas, or centres, deal with nerve messages going from or to different body parts.

## Control centres

You feel a touch on your skin. But where in your brain do the nerve messages end up?

movement
touch
taste
interpreting vision
vision (sight)
interpreting and choosing words
hearing
planning movements
anterior speech area
awareness

### NERVE TRAVEL UPDATE
- Most nerve messages have the same strength, about 0.1 volts. (About 1/15th the strength of a torch battery.)
- Some nerve messages travel quite slowly, just two metres per second.
- Others go much faster, over 100 metres per second.

16    **Body language**

**motor**   to do with movements, muscles, and the nerves controlling them
**sensory nerve**   nerve that takes messages from a sensor or sense organ to the brain

They go to the touch centre, which is a strap-shaped area of **cortex** running over the top of your brain, from one ear to the other. The touch centre is where your mind becomes aware of things touching your skin, and works out what they are.

## Making a move

Just in front of the touch centre is the **motor centre**. This is where you decide to make your movements and get them started.

There are many other centres in the cortex, each with a special job, like seeing, hearing, taste, understanding words and speaking.

## Centre problems

Sometimes a head injury affects the way the brain's centres work. For example, a person might suffer damage to the hearing centre in the cortex. Then he or she is unable to hear, even though the ears still work normally.

◀ Lights, sounds, smells, tastes and touches are detected by the body's **sense organs**. But it is only when the messages get to the brain that we become aware of them and understand what they mean.

**sense organs**    body parts, such as the nose, used in the senses

# Running on auto

## Automatic control

The brain stem has its own control centres for heartbeat, breathing, digesting food, altering the amount of blood flowing to different body parts, getting rid of wastes, and many other inner processes.

What have you done so far today? Run for the bus? Eaten breakfast? You probably didn't think of the most important things, like breathing, making your heart beat, and moving food through your guts! They seem to happen "by themselves", automatically without any thought on your part. Yet your brain controls them too.

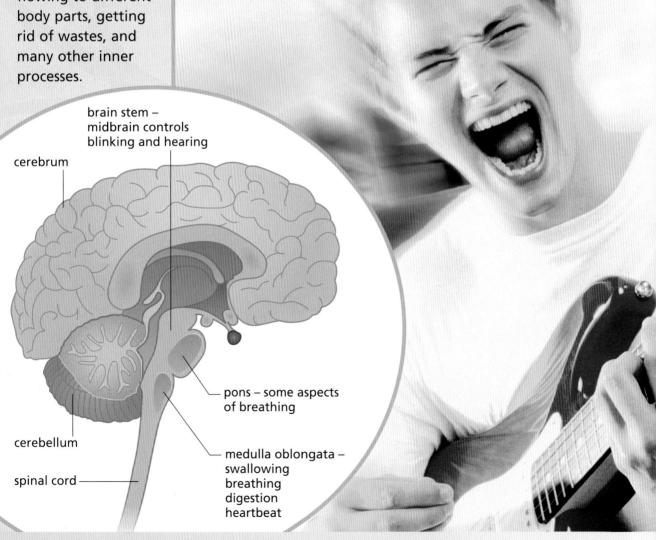

brain stem – midbrain controls blinking and hearing

cerebrum

cerebellum

spinal cord

pons – some aspects of breathing

medulla oblongata – swallowing breathing digestion heartbeat

**brain stem**   lowest part of the bain, where automatic actions are controlled

## Two brains in one?

Sometimes it might seem like you have two brains. You are aware of one – your thinking mind. You aren't aware of the other, which works by itself and controls things automatically. But all this happens in the same single brain.

The thinking mind is mainly based in the upper parts of the brain. Automatic control is carried out by the lower parts, mainly the **brain stem**. This is the stalk-like part at the base of the brain. Its lower end merges into the top of the body's main nerve, the **spinal cord**.

◄ Playing a musical instrument and singing at the same time is difficult. Imagine if you also had to remember to make your heart beat and your lungs breathe every second! Luckily the brain controls many body processes without you thinking about them.

### Burning up!

Body temperature is controlled by the brain's auto-system. But sometimes, if we fall ill, the control goes wrong. We get too hot, which is called a **fever**. We become sweaty and look red or flushed. We may need cooling with damp towels or a fan, until we feel better.

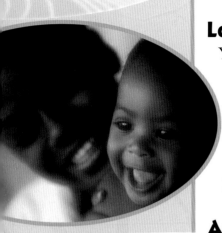

## Look out!!

You are sitting quietly, reading. Then suddenly – a big spider crawls across the page! Most people would react at once. Perhaps you would carefully put the book down so you don't harm the spider ... Or you may jump up and shout in panic! This shows how your brain can control fast reactions, and make your body go from resting still to leaping about in less than a second.

## Auto-reactions

Some types of body reactions happen and finish, even before you realize they have started. These are called **reflexes**. You probably blink your eyes over 30,000 times every day. Each blink is a reflex that washes away dirt and germs. If your nose gets blocked by dust, there's another reflex to clear it – sneezing. If you've eaten some bad food, then your stomach gets rid of it by another reflex, throwing up or vomiting.

## Bundles of reflexes

New babies haven't learned to control their bodies. Their actions are mainly reflexes. They cry if they are too hot, cold or hungry. They throw out their arms if you move them too fast or startle them. They fill their nappies at any time. Gradually as they grow, they learn to control these reflexes.

### TEST YOUR REACTIONS

Ask a friend to hold a ruler at the 30 cm (12 inch) end, so the zero end hangs down. Put your hands on either side of the ruler, level with its lower end. Your friend lets go, and you clap hands together to catch the ruler. The measurement where your hands touch the ruler indicates your reaction speed. Do your reactions get better with practice?

reflex   automatic reaction, such as coughing, or blinking

## Saved from danger

Reflexes help to keep you safe because they happen so fast. They take place immediately and automatically in your body, under the control of **nerve** circuits in that particular part. Then, slightly later, nerve messages pass to your brain, so you become aware of what has happened.

You may be deep in thought doing something else when you touch a sharp point or hot object. Your skin detects this, and before you fully realize what is happening, your reflexes move you away from the danger.

▼ If a fast-moving ball comes towards your head unexpectedly, you will automatically close your eyes, twist away and throw up your hands. These are all reflex reactions to protect your eyes and face. It is almost impossible not to flinch!

### Fast reactions

Reflexes happen very fast – but so do some of your conscious reactions! When sprinters begin a race, their ears hear the starting sound and pass the message to their brains. Then their brains send messages out to their leg muscles. The faster the sprinter's reactions, the better the chance of winning.

21

# Awake and asleep

For about one-third of your life, you are asleep. Does your brain switch off at this time? Not at all – it is just as busy as when you are awake. Millions of nerve signals pass around the sleeping brain, as they do in the waking brain. But they are different kinds of signals. The "brain-wave" lines of the **EEG** machine are different between waking and sleeping. Scientists know quite a lot about what happens in the brain during sleep. But there's still a great mystery about why we sleep.

## Yawn ...

Why do we yawn when we are tired, bored or just waking up? No one is really sure. Maybe we breathe less deeply when we feel tired. So we get less of the substance **oxygen**, which we need to stay alive. A yawn is an extra-deep breath that increases the amount of oxygen.

"Sleep testing" is often▶ used to try to solve the mysteries of our dreams and sleep patterns.

oxygen   gas which makes up one-fifth of air, and which the body needs

## Re-running the day

As you sleep, your body rests and saves energy. It repairs small amounts of normal wear and tear that happen every day. But what is your busy brain doing? Perhaps it goes through the events and memories of the day, like playing a recording. It sorts them into important or not. Then it can "forget" the less important ones, to leave memory space for the rest.

## Changing brainwaves

The up-and-down "brain waves" on the EEG machine change from fully awake, to daydreaming, feeling tired and dozy, and then fast asleep. In general the waves become taller and wider as we go from alert to asleep.

*At different times "brain waves" can be small...*

*... or tall and wide.*

23

## How much sleep?

On average, a new baby needs 18-20 hours of sleep, a ten-year-old needs 10-11 hours, and an adult needs 7-8 hours. But no one is "average" and we all need slightly different amounts of sleep. If we feel tired and can't concentrate by day, we're not getting enough sleep at night.

## Zzzzzz ...

When you go to sleep, you might not remember anything until morning. But your brain is very busy all night, and in different ways too.

When you first nod off, you soon go into deep **NREM sleep**. Your muscles are relaxed and floppy. Your heartbeat, breathing and other body processes slow down.

## Flickering eyes

But, after an hour or so, your muscles tense and twitch. In particular, your eyes flick to and fro, as though you are looking around an exciting scene, yet your eyelids stay closed. This is called **REM** (Rapid Eye Movement) **sleep**.

After another 30-60 minutes you go from REM sleep back to deep sleep (non-REM, or NREM sleep). These changes happen several times, from REM sleep to deep sleep and back again, until it is morning!

## Dreams

Do you dream much? Yes, you probably dream almost every night. But you may not remember your dreams.

People who are woken from REM sleep nearly always say they have been dreaming. They can usually recall their dreams. But people woken during deep sleep rarely recall any dreams. Like the puzzle of why we sleep, the reasons why we have deep and REM sleep, and why we dream, are still mostly a mystery.

NREM sleep   period of sleep when the body is very relaxed, the heartbeat and breathing are slow, there are no dreams, and it is difficult to wake up

## What if not?

Lack of sleep brings problems like headaches, poor concentration, loss of memory, clumsy movements, and bad moods. We are more likely to have accidents and suffer illnesses. A good night's sleep is one of our greatest health needs.

▲ Some people fall asleep almost anywhere. This is especially true when we are very young and active through the day, rushing about and playing and learning – or if we've had a late night.

"I woke up smelling smoke, looked out the window, and the house next door was on fire!"

Brett, 14, raised the alarm and his neighbours were saved from the fire. Thankfully, we don't switch off when we sleep. We still react to changes in our environment, like touches, smells or sounds.

**REM sleep**   period of sleep when the body is less relaxed, the heartbeat and breathing quicken, the eyes flicker, and dreams occur

# Sense-ational!

Are you sensitive? Of course, your body has five main **senses** These are eyes for sight, ears for hearing, nose for smell, tongue for taste, and skin for touch.

Each of these senses detects different types of changes in your surroundings and sends nerve messages to your brain. Your brain takes in all the information from your different senses and decides what to do.

## Inside the eye

The eye's pea-sized **lens** bends the light like a camera lens to give a clear, sharp view that shines onto the inner lining, the **retina**. This contains millions of microscopic cells. When light hits them, they send nerve messages to the brain.

## What a sight!

For most people, sight is the main sense for getting around, carrying out daily tasks and taking in information. The eye is specialized to change light into nerve messages – millions every second.

Light passes into the eye ➤ through the eye's clear **cornea**, then through the pupil, into the dark interior of the eyeball.

lens

iris

pupil

eye moving muscle

optic nerve

cornea

aqueous humour

ciliary muscle

retina

choroid

sclera

cornea   clear, dome-shaped front of the eye

About two-thirds of the information and knowledge in the brain comes in through the eyes, when we read words, and look at pictures, diagrams, photographs, screens, and real-life scenes.

## Bright eyes

Light shines into your eye through the dark hole or **pupil**. In dim light, your pupils open wide to let in as much light as possible. In bright light they shrink to reduce the amount of light getting in and protect the sensitive cells at the back of your eye.

## Security scan

The coloured part of the eye is a ring of muscle called the **iris**. It has a different pattern and colour in every person. The iris can be scanned or photographed for security, like fingerprints, to check identity.

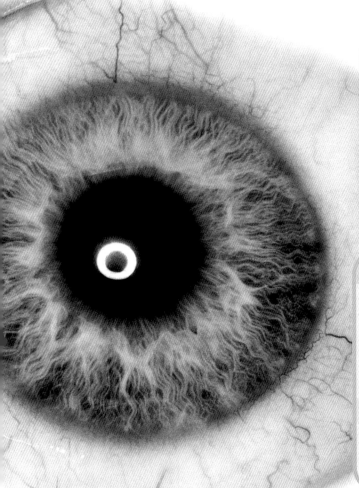

### EYE SEE!
- Your eyeball is about 2.5 cm across.
- Six tiny muscles behind the eye make it move to look up, down and to the side.
- The retina has more than 6 million cone cells. These see details and colours, but only work in bright light.
- The retina has more than 120 million microscopic cells called rods. These can only see shades of grey, but work well without much light.

**retina**   thin lining at the rear of the eyeball, that changes light ray patterns into patterns of nerve signals

## How you hear

Your ear is shaped to gather sound waves. They travel from outside into a tube, the ear canal. The waves bounce off the round eardrum, which vibrates. Movements pass along three tiny bones to the snail-shaped **cochlea**. Inside this, tiny cells change the vibrations into nerve messages and send these to the brain.

## All ears

Sit still and quiet, and listen hard. What can you hear? We are hardly ever in a silent place. There are usually sounds of some kind – people, traffic, machines, wind, rain, birds…

Your ears pick up these noises, and send **nerve** messages to your brain. But some sounds are just too quiet for our ears. Others are too high and shrill (**ultrasound**), or too low and deep (**infrasound**).

If you have pets like dogs, cats, rabbits and horses, you've probably noticed they have much better hearing than us. They prick up their ears at sounds that we can't hear at all.

We shut our eyes if light is too ➤ bright. We can only "shut" our ears to protect them from loud noises by putting our hands over them.

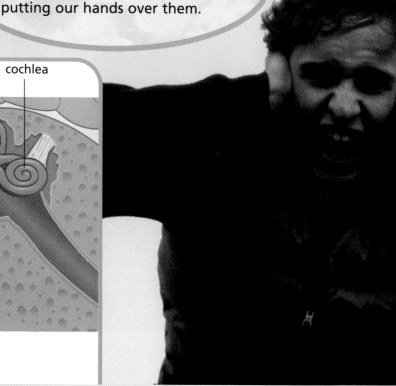

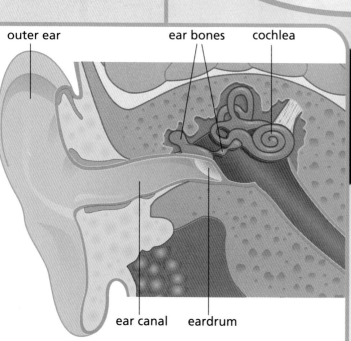

outer ear   ear bones   cochlea

ear canal   eardrum

cochlea   small, snail-shaped part in the ear, which changes movements or vibrations of sound into nerve messages

# Over here ... no, over there ...

Unlike animals, you can't prick up your ears. But like them, you can tell where a sound comes from.

Sounds travel as invisible "waves" through the air. These move at about 330 metres per second. If a sound comes from the right, it reaches your right ear about 1/1000th of a second before the left ear hears it. Sounds also lose loudness or volume as they travel. So the sound from the right is louder in your right ear than your left.

Your brain detects the tiny differences in time and loudness between your two ears, and works out the direction of a sound. This is called **stereophonic** hearing. For anyone deaf in one ear, this doesn't work.

## Well balanced

Some parts deep inside your ear do not detect sounds. They feel movements and the downward pull of gravity. They send nerve messages to your brain. Your brain combines this information with messages from your eyes, skin, muscles and joints. This helps you to keep your balance as you move about. Ear infections can make people lose their balance and feel dizzy.

## WARNING!

Too much loud noise can damage the delicate ear. There are laws for music clubs, work places, and bands about safe sound levels, which are measured in decibels (dB).

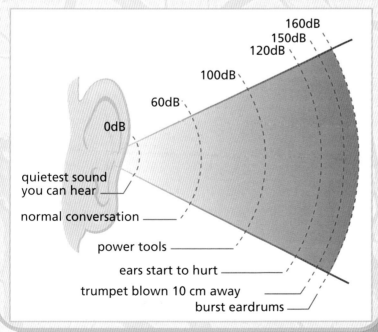

160dB
150dB
120dB
100dB
60dB
0dB

quietest sound you can hear
normal conversation
power tools
ears start to hurt
trumpet blown 10 cm away
burst eardrums

---

**stereophonic**   able to detect the direction of a sound because of slight differences in sound waves heard by the right and left ears

## Up your nose!

Your nostrils lead to two thumb-sized spaces inside, the **nasal chambers**. In their tops are two frilly-looking patches, each the size of a thumbnail. They contain 25 million tiny cells with very small hairs sticking from them.

When you breathe in, smelly particles in the air stick to the hairs, and the cells send nerve messages to the brain.

# Sniff ... what's that smell?

What was the last strong smell you remember? Flowers? Last night's dinner? Maybe perfume, the swimming pool, a sweaty changing room, a cleaning spray?

Smells can bring back strong memories and powerful feelings. This is because nerve messages from your nose go to parts of the brain involved in feelings, emotions and memories. Messages from other senses don't go direct to these parts.

# Why smells seem to fade

After you detect a strong smell, it seems to fade. But maybe it is still there, and just as strong.

Parts of your brain gradually stop the smell's nerve messages from going into your thoughts. This is because a smell you have already detected becomes less important, and you need to be aware of new smells instead.

# Keeping your mind clear

All of your sensory cells react in the same way. Think about the new sounds of a school or the feel of new shoes. After a while you don't notice them. This is called **habituation** and it is very helpful. It means your mind and thoughts aren't clogged up with old, unimportant information from your senses. Your thinking mind becomes aware only of new or changed sensations.

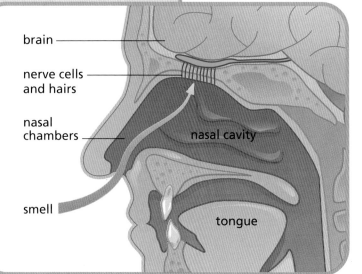

brain

nerve cells and hairs

nasal chambers

nasal cavity

smell

tongue

30    **Body language**    habituation   when senses get used to something and do not seem to detect it any more

We hate the smells that come from rotten food, old rubbish, manure and animal droppings. This is helpful – our senses are warning us to stay away from these smells. Otherwise we could catch germs and disease.

## Good or bad?

What do you love to smell, and what do you hate? Put these smells in a list, from good to bad. Ask your friends to do the same. Did you all make the same choices?

vinegar

strong cheese

fresh bread

boiled cabbage

oranges

camp-fire smoke

chocolate sauce

garlic

just-mowed grass

Dear Kyle,

I suddenly thought of you the other day. I was camping, and the smell of the tents and bacon cooking over the gas stove took me straight back to that summer camp we went on when we were nine...

**nasal chambers** hollow parts between the nostrils and upper throat, where smells are detected

## It is on the tip of my tongue

Different parts of your tongue are thought to detect different flavours. The tip senses sugary tastes best, like sweets and chocolate. You detect bitter tastes, like tonic water or coffee, as you swallow and the food passes over the back of your tongue.

## Terrific tastes

Can you remember the flavours of your food yesterday? Sometimes we rush to eat, and hardly taste a thing. If we take more time, we can enjoy food's tastes, its textures – crunchy, flaky, lumpy or creamy – and its temperature. These feelings of texture and temperature come from the sense of touch inside your mouth.

As you are chewing, smells from the food pass up the back of your mouth into your nose chamber, to your smell sensors. So what you think of as "taste" is really your senses of taste, smell and touch all working together.

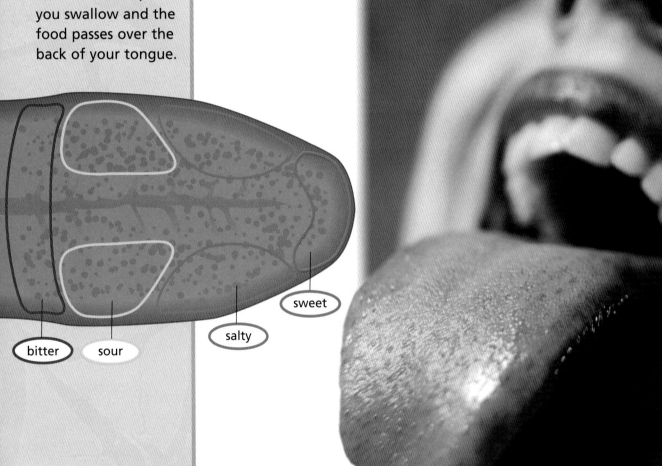

bitter   sour   salty   sweet

**Body language**   papillae   small lumps, for example, on the surface of the tongue

## Tongue's tasks

Your tongue doesn't just taste your food. It moves the food around inside your mouth, so you can chew it properly. You've seen the tiny bumps all over your tongue, called **papillae**. These help to grip the slippery food.

Your tongue also licks food and dribbles off your lips. And it moves when you talk, so you can speak words clearly. Try saying "hello" without moving your tongue!

### TASTE CHALLENGE

Some scientists believe that the tongue has different taste areas, but others have doubts. What do you think? Ask a friend to close their eyes, and with a clean spoon, put a small amount of sugar on the tip of their tongue. Can they tell it is sugar?

After a water mouthwash, try salt on the tongue tip. Can they guess what it is, or do they need to move it to another area of the tongue to recognise the salty taste?

### Don't be silly, it tastes lovely!

Taste buds gradually die away over the years. So tastes and flavours seem stronger for young people compared to older people. Also breathing in fumes or smoke, as you do if you smoke cigarettes, damages your taste buds, and makes flavours "dull".

◄ You taste with your tongue's 10,000 **taste buds**, beside and between the papillae. Taste buds are far too small to see, shaped like tiny oranges made of microscopic cells, with hairs sticking out. Taste particles in food stick to the hairs and the cells send nerve messages to the brain.

**tastebuds**   ball-shaped groups of cells on the tongue that detect tastes

## Inside skin

Touch is detected by micro-sensors just under skin's surface layer. They send nerve messages to the brain. Disc-shaped sensors near the surface feel light touch. Blob-shaped ones lower down sense pressure. Branched ones, like tiny trees, detect pain.

## Getting in touch

The sense based in your skin is called touch. But it detects far more than being touched.

Imagine your eyes are closed and you have to guess what an object is, by touch alone. You feel very carefully for its shape and size. Is its surface smooth or lumpy, slippery or rough? Are there any edges or ridges? You press to see if the object is hard or soft. You can also detect if it is warm or cold, and perhaps wet or dry.

Your skin senses these many different features. So touch is not as simple as it seems!

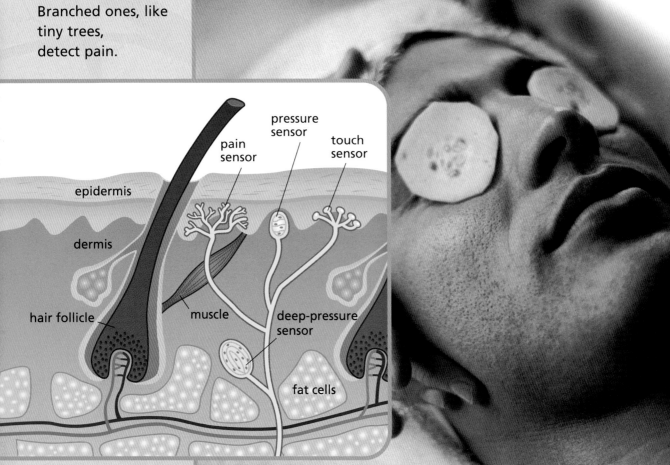

epidermis

dermis

hair follicle

pain sensor

pressure sensor

touch sensor

muscle

deep-pressure sensor

fat cells

**micro-sensors**  microscopic nerve endings in skin, which detect the various features of touch

## Fingertips and lips

If you try the test, you would probably use your fingers. These are very sensitive for touch. Your eyelids, lips and tongue are also very sensitive.

All these areas have lots of the **micro-sensors** that detect touch. One fingertip has more than 3,000 micro-sensors packed close together. Other areas of skin, like the lower back and front thigh, have fewer micro-sensors, so they are less touch-sensitive.

## Ouch!

Skin has another sense, which we don't like – pain. But we need pain. It warns if our skin and the body underneath are getting damaged. Then we can take care to prevent any more harm, keep protected and help healing.

## DID YOU KNOW?

Hairs cannot feel touch as they are dead. (Otherwise a haircut would be very painful!) However each hair has micro-sensors around its base in the skin. These sense the hair being pulled or moved. Sometimes when you feel a "touch", nothing contacts your skin. You are feeling your tiny body hairs being moved.

## Itchy-scratchy

Why does skin feel an itch? It might be a tiny insect walking or biting, like a mosquito. It could be one of skin's tiny hairs, bent over and rubbing the surface. It may be bits of dust from the air setting off the micro-sensors. A quick scratch usually works, but itching caused by an illness, like a rash, may need to be seen by the doctor.

◄ Touch affects our mood. Some kinds can be very soothing, like a gentle massage or stroking. Other touches are strange, funny, or scary.

# Chemical control

Your brain is your body's boss. It controls most body parts by sending messages along **nerves**. But there is another control system too. This is based, not on nerve messages, but natural body chemicals called **hormones**.

Your mind is not aware of how hormones are made or work. But you often feel their effects. When you are very frightened, thirsty or worried, hormones are involved. They also control how the body grows, and how it repairs damage.

In general, hormones are in charge of slow processes that take from hours to weeks and years, like growing. Nerves control faster process that happen in seconds or minutes, like movement.

## Hormone glands

Some hormone glands make just one hormone. Others produce several. A few body parts make hormones in addition to their main jobs. These include the heart and stomach.

**The body parts that make hormones**

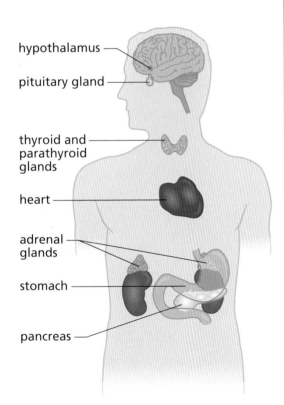

- hypothalamus
- pituitary gland
- thyroid and parathyroid glands
- heart
- adrenal glands
- stomach
- pancreas

**target organs**   body parts affected by a certain hormone. The heart is one of adrenaline's target organs.

## Where are hormones made?

There are dozens of hormones, each affecting different body processes. They are made in about ten **endocrine glands.** Your blood stream carries the hormones from these glands all around your body. As they reach certain body parts, they control how those parts work.

In general, more hormone makes the part work faster. Together the brain, nerves and hormones keep all your body parts working together.

## HORMONES ON TARGET

- Each hormone controls certain body parts, called its target organs.
- Certain hormones have just a few target organs, like the heart or stomach.
- Other hormones affect almost every microscopic cell. The whole body is their target.

## Nerves and stress

When we feel nervous, anxious or worried, this is partly the result of more hormones in the blood. These stress hormones put us "on edge". These are some of the fast acting hormones.

◄ Hormones control water in the body. If there is too much, they make the extra water pass into urine. If there is not enough water, hormones reduce the amount of urine, and your brain tells you that you are thirsty.

## Twin tasks

The **pancreas**, behind the stomach, has two main jobs. One is to make powerful juices that digest food in the guts. The other is making two hormones, insulin and glucagon. These control the glucose sugar in the blood – your main source of energy.

## Little yet big

Sometimes small things can be very important. This is true of your **pituitary**. It is behind your eyes, at the lower front of your brain, and only the size of a kidney bean. Yet it makes more than ten **hormones**. Most of these control how other hormone glands work. So your pituitary is the boss of your whole hormone system.

## Double control

However, your pituitary does not work by itself. It is joined by a narrow stalk to the brain part above it called the **hypothalamus**. Mentioned earlier in the book, this is involved in powerful feelings and emotions like anger, fear and joy.

Nerve signals and chemical substances pass from the hypothalamus along the stalk to the pituitary and tell it when to set free its hormones. This is how your body's two main control systems, nerves and hormones, are linked.

The pituitary (seen from the ➤ front in this brain scan) is linked to the brain by a thin strip or stalk. Messages pass along this as **nerve signals** and hormone-like chemicals, so here the nerve system and hormone system work together.

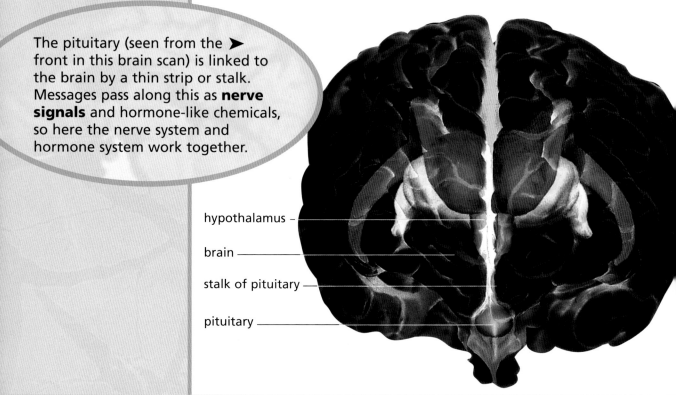

hypothalamus

brain

stalk of pituitary

pituitary

pancreas   part that makes juices for digestion, and hormones to control the level of blood glucose

## In the neck

The **thyroid** in your neck makes hormones to control how fast your body's millions of microscopic cells work. If the thyroid goes wrong, the whole body slows down and feels very tired, or speeds up and works too fast. Usually these problems can be treated with medicines.

Dear Diary,

Today I told my school friends I have diabetes, which means my pancreas doesn't make enough of the hormone insulin. So my blood sugar isn't controlled properly. I need to inject insulin at certain times. Otherwise I would feel faint, and might collapse. Now my friends understand why I need the injections.

◄ People with diabetes may need regular injections, and also have to be be careful about what they eat.

**pituitary** the main endocrine or hormone-making gland in the brain
**thyroid** endocrine or hormone-making gland in the neck

## Run for it!

BOO! Has something frightened you lately?

When you are surprised or afraid, do you feel your heart thumping and 'butterflies' in your stomach? Your skin goes sweaty and your muscles tense, ready for fast movement. These changes are partly the result of nerve messages, and partly due to the hormone called **adrenaline**.

Some people like the ➤ excitement of being scared, especially when they know they are safe really. These feeling are brought on by nerves and also by the hormone adrenaline.

## Through the "pain barrier"

Some athletes carry on even when they are exhausted or injured. They don't seem to notice the hardship and pain. This is due to the effects of adrenaline and other hormones. Their nerves may tell them to stop because of pain, but their hormones and willpower say "keep going".

adrenals  two glands, one on top of each kidney, which make several hormones including adrenaline

## A big buzz

Adrenaline is made in your **adrenals**, two hormone glands on top of your kidneys. Adrenaline works with your brain and nerves to get your body ready for action. For example, it changes the way blood flows around your body. Less blood flows to your skin and to your stomach and guts, and more blood rushes to the muscles you would use to run away!

This is why, when you are scared, your skin turns pale, and you feel a tightening or fluttering inside your stomach.

## Water, energy, stress, repair

The adrenals make other hormones as well as adrenaline. These other hormones affect growth, alter the amount of water in urine, help to control blood sugar for energy, and help body parts to cope with stress and repair everyday wear-and-tear.

The affects of adrenaline and nerves cause the "fight or flight" reaction. Your body makes itself ready to battle with danger, or fly ... that is, run away.

- Heart beats faster
- Lungs breathe faster and deeper
- More blood flows to muscles
- Less blood flows to other body parts (skin, intestines, and so on)
- Pupils of eyes open wide
- Skin sweats
- Tiny hairs in skin stand on end, making goosebumps
- Senses become extra-alert
- Brain prepares to make fast decisions

## Changing bones

Growing does not just mean getting bigger. Inside the body, as the bones of the skeleton grow, they change shape and become harder. This is another long, slow process controlled mainly by hormones.

## Oh, grow up!

You can click your fingers in a second. Fast actions like this are usually controlled by **nerves**. But growing from a baby to an adult takes about 20 years. Slow processes are controlled by **hormones**. The main hormone affecting growth is called growth hormone. It comes from the chief hormone gland, the **pituitary** under the brain.

## Up and up

Our full-grown body height, when we are adults, is controlled mainly by the **genes** we inherit from our parents. But how fast we grow to this adult height is partly due to growth hormone.

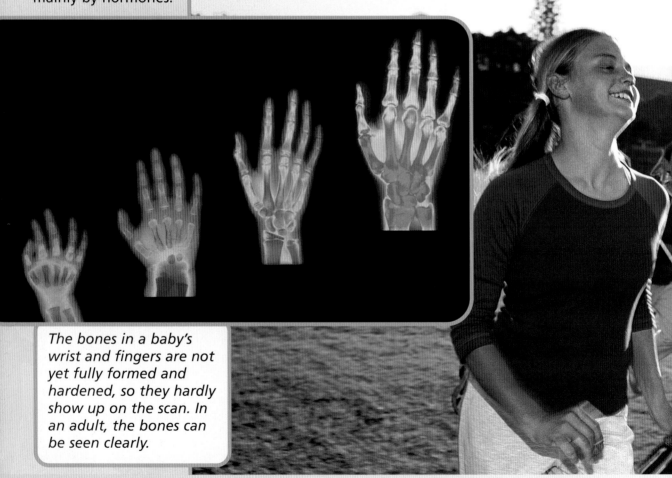

*The bones in a baby's wrist and fingers are not yet fully formed and hardened, so they hardly show up on the scan. In an adult, the bones can be seen clearly.*

**genes**   instructions for how the body grows, develops, and works

Some people naturally have slightly more of it. So they grow faster and reach their adult height younger, compared to those with slightly less growth hormone. This is all part of the normal, natural differences between people.

## Too much, too little

In very rare cases, the pituitary makes too much growth hormone by mistake. Then the body grows extra-fast. Or the pituitary makes too little, and the body stays small. Luckily these problems are soon noticed, and can be treated by medicines.

▼ These young people are all about the same age. But they are different heights, partly due to the effects of growth hormone.

### Yes, master
The human brain does not work as fast or have as much memory as some computers. Also the body's control system of **nerves** and hormones is not always perfect. But imagine a robot with a supercomputer brain and a perfect machine-like body. It would always be right and never go wrong. It could soon become very boring!

# Find out more

## Where to search

### Search engine
A search engine looks through the entire web and lists all sites that match the words in the search box. It can give thousands of links, but the best matches are at the top of the list, on the first page. Try **bbc.co.uk/search**

### Search directory
A search directory is like a library of websites that have been sorted by a person instead of a computer. You can search by keyword or subject and browse through the different sites like you look through books on a library shelf. A good example is **yahooligans.com**

## Books
*Brain: Injury, Illness and Health* Steve Parker (Heinemann Library, 2003)

*Spinal Cord and Nerves: Injury, Illness and Health* Steve Parker (Heinemann Library, 2003)

*Body: An Amazing Tour of Human Anatomy* Robert Winston (Dorling Kindersley, 2005)

*The Brain: Our Nervous System* Seymour Simon (Sagebrush, 2001

## World Wide Web
If you want to find out more about muscles and bones, you can search the Internet using keywords like these:
- 'fight or flight'  - eardrum + decibels  - retina

You can also find your own keywords by using headings or words from this book. Use the search tips below to help you find the most useful websites.

## Search tips
There are billions of pages on the Internet so it can be difficult to find exactly what you are looking for. These search skills will help you find useful sites quickly:

- Use simple keywords instead of whole sentences
- Use two to six keywords in a search, putting the most important words first
- Be precise – only use names of people, places or things
- If you want to find words that go together, put quote marks around them, for example 'stomach acid'.
- Use the advanced section of your search engine
- Use the + sign between keywords to link them, for example typing + KS3 after your keyword will help you find web pages at the right level.

# Glossary

**adrenaline**  hormone that gets the body ready for action

**adrenals**  two glands, one on top of each kidney, which make several hormones including adrenaline

**axon**  part of a nerve cell (neuron) that takes nerve signals from the main cell body to other nerve cells or to muscles or glands

**blood glucose**  sugar obtained from the breakdown of other sugars and carbohydrates in food – the body's main source of energy

**brain stem**  lowest part of the brain, where automatic actions are controlled

**cells** microscopic "building blocks" which make up all body parts

**cerebellum** part at the rear of the brain, which controls muscle actions

**cerebral cortex**  thin grey layer covering the cerebrum (main upper part of the brain), involved in thinking, memory, experiencing the surroundings through the senses, planning movements and many other mental activities

**cerebral hemispheres**  two halves of the cerebrum

**cerebrum**  large upper portion of the brain, with "white matter" of nerve fibres inside, and a surface layer of "grey matter" or nerve cells called the cerebral cortex.

**cochlea**  small snail-shaped part in the ear, which changes movements or vibrations of sound into nerve messages.

**cornea**  clear dome-shaped front of the eye

**CSF**  cerebrospinal fluid

**dendrites**  parts that take messages from nerve cells to the main cell body

**EEG** electro-encephalogram

**endocrine glands**  parts that make hormones

**fever**  raised body temperature, when the person may feel hot and sweaty, or cold and shivery

**genes**  instructions for how the body grows, develops, and works

**glucagon**  hormone made by the pancreas, which raises the level of blood glucose

**hippocampus**  part inside the brain that is important for memory

**hormones**  substances made by hormonal or endocrine glands, which spread around the body in the blood and affect or control body parts

**hypothalamus**  small part of the brain that deals with emotions and automatic processes

**infrasound**  sounds which are too low for a human to hear

**insulin** hormone made by the pancreas, which lowers the level of blood sugar/glucose

**iris** ring of muscle at the front of the eye, between the white part and the pupil, which gives the eye its colour

**lens** the pea-sized part behind the pupil which bends or focuses light into the inside of the eyeball

**meninges** three thin layers around the brain and spinal cord, which protect and nourish them. They are called the dura mater, arachnoid, and pia mater

**micro-sensors** microscopic nerve endings in skin, which detect the various features of touch

**motor** to do with movements, muscles, and the nerves controlling them

**motor centre** strap-shaped region on brain's cerebral cortex, which is in control of muscle movements

**nasal chambers** hollow parts between the nostrils and the upper throat, where smells are detected

**nerve cell** cell specialized to receive, process, and sendon nerve messages as tiny pulses of electricity

**nerves** string-like parts that carry messages around the body as tiny pulses of electricity

**NREM sleep** (non-REM sleep) period of sleep when the body is very relaxed, the heartbeat and breathing are slow, there are no dreams, and it is difficult to wake up

**oxygen** gas which makes up one-fifth of air, and which the body needs

**papillae** small lumps, for example, on the surface of the tongue.

**pituitary** the main endocrine or hormone-making gland below the brain

**pupil** hole in the middle of the eye though which light enters

**reflex** automatic reaction such as coughing, or blinking

**REM** (Rapid Eye Movement) sleep period when the body is less relaxed, the heartbeat and breathing quicken, the eyes flicker, and dreams occur

**retina** thin lining at the rear of the eyeball, which changes light ray patterns into patterns of nerve signals

**sciatic nerve** the main nerve in each side of the lower back, hip and upper leg, carrying messages between the leg and the spinal cord

**sense organs** body parts, such as the nose, used in the senses

**senses** the ability of the body to detect something such as light, temperature or the level of a certain substance inside itself, and send messages to the brain

**sensor** a part which detects something, like light, sound, or the level of a certain substance inside itself, and sends messages to the brain

**sensory nerve** nerve which carries messages from a sensor or sense organ, like the eye or skin, to the brain

**skull** main bone in the head, which is really more than 20 bones joined together

**spinal cord** main nerve linking the brain to the rest of the body

**stereophonic** able to detect the direction of a sound because of the slight differences in sound waves heard by the left and right ears

**target organs** body parts affected by a certain hormone. The heart is one of adrenaline's target organs, and beats faster and stronger when adrenaline levels rise

**taste buds** ball-shaped groups of cells on the tongue that detect tastes

**thalamus** parts in the brain, involved in awareness, sensing the surroundings, memory and other mental activities

**thyroid** endocrine or hormone making gland in the neck

**ultrasound** sounds which are too high for a human to hear

**ventricles** spaces inside a body part, such as the four ventricles inside the brain, which are filled with cerebrospinal fluid

# Index